BE BEAUTIFUL

♥

Written by
Jennifer Circosta

You are a Powerful Experience

∞

Also Written by Jennifer Circosta

1713 Maplewood Drive
∞

The Many Tails of Luck-shmee
∞

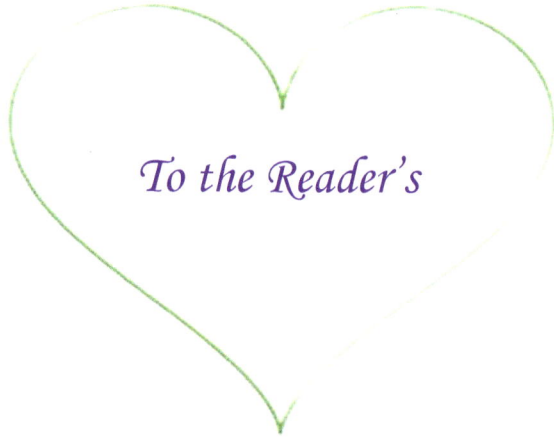

To the Reader's

This is an Invitation to Open Your Hearts

BE
BEAUTIFUL

Is a Collection of Dialogue and Poetry that Reflects our
Universal Experiences of Sensuality and Beauty.

It Speaks of our Interactions with the
Elements of Nature & Our Reach for Spiritual Connection.

BE
BEAUTIFUL

Is an ArTistic EmOtional eXpression of
Pure Energy and Captures the Light of Life!

The Muse Melts the Flesh and Transcends the Spirit~
Step into the Labyrinth of Poetry and Find Yourself

∞

Table of Concepts

Let Us Begin

Let us Begin
        With~

PASSION

Let us Always
        Begin,
            With~

PASSION

That Fire
Burning~
In the pit of your belly

A Motion
Constant-
In your mind

A Desire
Smoldering~
Inside you

A Perpetual Force-
        An Explosion of Creativity!

That Moves you,
        That Drives you ~ ~ ~

Deeper

&

Deeper

Into Who You Really Are

YOU AWAKEN…

PASSION

Let Me

Let Me
>   Steal~
Those kisses from your mouth
That you say are mine

Let Me
>   Journey~
Beside expression's palette

Skin- - -
>   - - -Scarlet

Flushed Love Fusion

Let Me
>   Roll~
Over supple valleys
Climb,
Pink- - -
>   - - -Flesh
Tender
>   Touch,
Crest of lunar light

~ All the while ~

Chasing
>   One,

Dainty
>   Kiss,

After
>   Another...

Dare Me...

Lips- - -
          - - -Soft
Gliding along urge~
Descending
          Down,
Nape of neck-
Burrowing indulgence

Let Me
          Calm~
Quite
Cradled-
Inside your grip of Grace
Granting- - -
               - - -Forbidden
Fond
    Fingertips~
To Tip
          Toe,
Toward-
          Twists and Twirls

~ ~ ~ ~ Sinking Deep ~ ~ ~ ~

In Humming Labyrinth

Gaze me
          Silence...
Universe of your Soul-

Eye to Eye
And
I to I

Take flight within me~

Body to Body

Let Us
BE

Breath to Breath

Let Us
Beat to Rhythm

Heart to Heart

Let Us
Deep Within

Pulse to Pulse

Let Us
Pulse to Pulse

Pulse to Pulse

Let Us
Pulse to Pulse

Pulse to Pulse

Let Us

~ Pulse ~

…to pulse

to pulse…

5

When I write,

I FEEL

I Feel
For the Sounds of words

I Feel them-

INSIDE

Welling Toward Wit
      And
Bending,
      Broken Heart-

I SENSE THEM

I Assimilate
And
Digest Them-

Swirling
     Spinning,

~ ~ ~ MOVEMENT ~ ~ ~

Striking!
     Words
Inside-

VOCALIZE

HARMONIZE

Tis` but a Language of-

HEART

Tis` but a Language of-

SOUL

Tis` but a Breath of-

LIFE

So let us Listen~

Let us Hear-

Let us,

BE STILL~

INSIDE

EXPANSION

Look Up!

The sky is cloudy
The trees-
Bare

Mist
Hangs heavy-
Pregnant and perched
In crisp grey air
Dew drops
        Dangle,
From nude
        Bronze branches
The surroundings,
Are gloomy
But-
The ground promises
New Life!

Bright little buds
Bursting!
Yellow sun
Seeping
Through blood of optimism-
Green blades
Rising
In hearts of hope!

~ Centered Deep ~

In time and rhythm
Spreading-
Tiny blooms of violet hues and pansy smiles

I look up
To the grey sullen sky
Cast in cloudy-pale lackluster

In the evaporation
Of isolation,
      I contemplate-
The transformations of this world- -
Its molten raven tempers!
Against-
Blue… Phlegmatic… Phases…

Its fruitless tapestries
~ Exposed ~
Against
Explosions of fertility!

Its Death-
Rebirth-
Its Courage-
      To Survive!

It is an innate knowing,
The willingness-
To Live!

Look Up

Is it just the sky…
Or are we viewing what lies behind the eyes echo?

Is it just the sky…
Or are we observing the pits and falls,
The trials and triumphs of human ways?

Is it just the sky…
Or are we looking into the lens
Into the soul-
Of something greater
Yet,
That which we aspire to be?

To Become-

Look Up...

Is it really just the sky…?

I think-
I feel-
I stand here

Now-
In This Moment,

- Suspended -

Silent
Still-
Carried high,

Higher,

Highest,

Within The Force of Life!

I know-
It's not just the sky…

I Know

I AM

We are Curious people, aren't we?
We Crave Knowledge
Understanding-
We Want to Know

- TO DISCOVER -

Look Inside-
      And Discover

DISCOVER YOURSELF

Experience Yourself in the Moment
In THIS Moment-

Feel,

      A Shift-

Feel…

… CHANGE …

We are Constant Change-
Experiences Change,
      Thoughts Change-
Emotions Change,
      People Change-

We Change!
As Individuals
As Creative Beings

WE CHOOSE
WE CHANGE

Change/Choice
Choice/Change

CHOOSE

Be Changed-

CHOOSE

Cause Change-

Life is changeable. . .

Water

The center of my womb
Opens forward-
Petals
Orange blossom
Pleasure and flow exchange
Feelings Arise
For sweetness-
To enter and subsist within me

Seed and suckling
Evergreen earth
Ascending-
Fertile persuasions pounding
- Against -
Rumbling roars of crimson flames!
      Fractured forms-
Of night filled light
- Bedspread
Deep... Indigo... Calm...

And with a thousand claps of thunder!
Crackling-
Compelling Ardor Shatters!
     Collapsing-
         Cleansing-
Particles of light and sound

Let Me   =   Absorb You

Receive me-
Into you
Into the ground-
Into your roots-
Your tissues,
And cells

The sustenance of blood and flesh

~ Balance ~

Within circulating compounds
Throbbing-
Through vessels of infinity

I AM Life!

The springs of legendary tales
Bottled-
In the imaginations of men
Pliable-
In the buoyancy of babes
Playfully,
        Lapping,
Along ripples of smiles
Silent sighs-
        Lull you,
To still and slumber
Quiet…
        Silence-
Surrounds
Submerged bodies
Intertwine-
Become One

Channeling
        Changes-
Now,
Watch me
        Fall,
From cliffs
        With white capped tops
Smoothing,
        The rocks below
Just to capture,
        The spark and *twinkle* of Iris

*I **Rise** in **Lover's Eyes**...*

Go on,
Take my full body
Solid-
Sizzling a top skin
      Gliding,
Along peaks and slithering
      Down,
         Slopes
Ahhhhh….

Refreshing-
      Laughter!

The laughter you share-
Slipping
      And
         Sliding
On the surface of my belly
With the *sparkles* of frost
Signaling the moon,
To shine brightly in the night!

Mittens on and rosy cheeks
I keep you a float
Below your feet-
And the chill in the air…

Brings warm hearts together

I AM

Your Reflection~

Look Inside…

It's Time…

NOW

Is the Time-

-It's Time

TIME

To Capture-

A Moment
An Instant-
An Occasion!

TO LAUGH!

To Release
A Relief-
A Respite!

~ LAUGHTER ~

Look at the person next to you-

LAUGH!

Look up at the ceiling-

LAUGH!

Look inside your heart-

AND

LAUGH!

19

FEEL…

Feel the Ecstasy of Pure Joy
Inside you

Feeding you-

      Imagine…

Sitting in the Belly of Laughter!
Being tickled,
By its Sound Current

It's Time-

NOW

-Is the Time For-

IN-JOY!

The country road

      Spreads wide~

           Even wider ahead of me…

My presence is embraced by its vast point of view and my
leisure ambulation welcomes calm pathways…

I hear the pop!
      Crackling,
Sounds of baby pebbles and stones
Retorting-
Against the soles of my pink and white sneakers

I gaze ahead~
      Above trees,
Through open spaces - - between leaves
To witness,
In the distance-
That my search for elation
Is indeed within my reach
I Am
Attuned to its entreaty

My journey toward
Joy
Begins-
Alongside the autumn breeze
Its speech
      Clamors-
Through my blue windbreaker
Whipping
      And
         Whirling
In its native tongue

The Wind moves
        Changes,
Shape and speed
        As she whispers
A sweet song…
And my caramel highlights
Lift!
        And
                Twirl
In flight!
        Flitting by~
Long Lashes,
Melting… Dark… Chocolate… Eyes…

Sun Splashes
Bright!
Contagious light-
Yellow and Bronze tones
Splendor-
The template of Mother Nature
They cover her frame
Yet-
Reveal Her playful tenor

As Leaves
        Drop,

Blue sky
        Falls,

Wistful~
        ~Wishes

Wearing garments
In varying shades of October light-

My eyes delight!

IN-JOY!

Evergreen brush sways thick
As chill air
Strikes!
Tiny bloom-blossom
Purple bud
Magnified-
By a thousand suns!
          With just a dust~
Of golden streaks on pretty petals
Her face
- Bold -
Dazzling
A delicate expression,

IN-JOY!

Rhythmic currents
          Shift-
Tunnels of rumbles
Whisper-
          -Whiskered
Yellow Puckered Pine
Towering-
In lush beauty and hearty innocence

I Stop-

I Open-

I Give-

To Mother Nature and Her Beloved

~ Balancing ~
          Inside the pause-

A space

          - Between -

The vibrations of Grace
        Generating Sensations
Through ageless bristles
His Majesty,
Moves briskly by-
Like a thousand tiny fingers
Tickling Visage Way

The breeze picks up
Swirling through~
Filling spaces - - between - - thick branches
And clusters of crunchy leaves
It carry's the blue-tailed bird

ABOVE

While-

BELOW

A game of hide and seek plays
I hear the Chirp!
        Chirp!
           Tweet!
Of a bird on the ground I can't find
Yet, I know…

Look!
   Over there-
A Woolly Bear…
Wonders by my feet
Slowly - - - Scrunching - - Body - By
Along his solitary path
- Concealed -
In his fuzzy *Black* and *Orange* Halloween Costume

My heart-
      Softens,
She welcomes a greater space-

I Am Connecting
To ALL that is,

And ALL that is,
Sustains me~

IN-JOY!

Think about it?
Ask yourself…

WHAT BRINGS YOU JOY?

To Give
To Receive
To Share

To Play,
        Like Children-

Innocent
        Pure-

DO WE REMEMBER?

Do we Remember How...?
To Simply
Be-
Like Children?

Bright Eyes
Small Hands
Big Hearts!

Open!
Ready-
Willing~

To Give
To Receive
To Share-

LOVE

LOVE

We *ALL*
Search for it

LOVE

We *ALL*
Welcome it
    When it Strikes!

LOVE

And We
    - ALL -
Mourn it - - - - when it's gone

LOVE

May come and go sometimes
But we never give up on it, right…?
In fact, We Never-
Truly give up on any of these concepts we share

. PASSION .

. EXPANSION .

. CHOICE .

These Single Words
That Describe our Feelings-

. LAUGHTER .

. JOY .

. LOVE .

29

No-
We Hold on to Them
They Breathe Inside of Us
It is the Substance
That Fuels us,
That Catapults us Forward!

To be Creative

TO CREATE

No Judgments-
No Stopping of Self-

JUST.

PURE.

CREATION.

To See
To Hear
To Feel
To Touch-

To Be Touched…

THE - SENSES - CONNECT - US

We ALL Desire

CONNECTION

To Be Connected
To be a part of
Something-
To Be
    Somebody…

To Connect to Others

To Our Work,
                To Our Purpose-

And Most Importantly,
                To Ourselves…

To Connect with Yourself
Who You Truly Are,
Is Amazing and Unstoppable-

CONNECTION

Amethyst

My eyes gaze
Sparkles
Into the deep purple hues
Resting-
Within the core of your belly

My mind,
      Poised-
             Dives~

… Ego First …

Into the abyss of Understanding
That I may stand under-
The mere perceptions of this world

I Rise up!
From mineral and stone
And open self to the vastness
Of the midnight sky
        Wrapped-
In the blanket of stillness…

I AM
Dissolving-
      Vanishing~
Into the deep Indigo maze of your jagged frame
Shattered!
By the crisp tones of your Brilliance

... Captivate Me...

... Penetrate Me...

... Haunt Me...

Make my Two Eyes
Three-

Dazzle me
Spectacle of Truth!

I Am Aware

To be Aware
Is to Shed the Skins of Innocence
And Plant your Roots
In the Tower of Wisdom

THE HEART

Wants you…

It taps you on the Shoulder
It Calls You,
          It Beckons-
It Pleads with you…
It says,

(((OPEN ME)))

And

… SET ME FREE …

AHHHH… ANAHATA…

It is the Heart's Name
          The Eternal Beat~
The Pump-
          Of Devotion

AHHHH… ANAHATA…

It is an Endless Rhythm
A Motion-
          The Flame~
               Of Desire!

ANAHATA…

She is Sweet Benevolence!
The Knowing
          Of Self-
The seat of your Destiny
          The Internal Glow
That is YOU!

… Your Heart …

Whispers Your Name
And You Have to
You Must-

Let it Fly...

Call Me

You Call me once
You Call me twice
My God,
Call me until I answer!

You've comforted me
And made me see
The sight-
That bird's take flight

I hear the bells
That beckon me
A song sung
From your dove to me

I'll fall asleep
To this song so deep
'Tis mine,
A sweet lullaby to keep

You draw me near
The love that's here
Begins to ease
My slightest fear

I see the twinkles
And appear my angels
I realize-
To my surprise,
My time has come
And will arise

My eyes open wide
The feeling inside
… Astounding…

To witness this painting before me
I sit and I stare
I begin to wonder where
My Lord,
Where are you and do you even care...?

I speak to the clouds
In hopes that you'll hear
This message from my heart-

I say aloud,
Lord hear my sound
From you,
I will not part

Shine your light
Make it right
And guide me through your door-
Listen Lord,
I speak out loud
`Tis nobler then a pun-
As I run I say to thee,
"Thy will shall be done!"

You've paved my path
You've made it straight
I see your eyes of gold

The crown you wear
You pass to me
For I-
To have and to hold

My eyes open wider
My heart has opened
In you,
I do delight

You've made me as I started
...Whole...

Now to you,
Sweet Lord I go-

I gallop to your loving arms
With wings upon my feet
The thought you might console me,
When at first we meet

I've come My Lord,
I stand here naked
Unashamed as can be-
So take me there
To I don't know where
But your love is what I need

Now I see
Why you've come for me-
My Lord,
You're here-
To set me free!

You taught me well
You gave me sight-
Now I know
I AM
That bird in flight!

Please dear Lord
Let's do this right
Just hold me close
And hold me tight-

Oh my God!
It's really me…

Now I see-

. . . .

. . . .

I'm finally free …

40

FREEDOM

Freedom to Think-
       To Feel
To Express
       To Communicate
To Be-

TO BECOME

As You Are
How You Are
When You Are

To Be-

YOURSELF

Simply
Completely-

In the Moment

IN THIS MOMENT

Right Now-

…BREATHE…

..FEEL..

.BE.

AUTHENTICITY

Authenticity-
Is a True Freedom
A Power
     And
       A Privilege-

When you Create from
       That Space-

When you are that Honest with yourself
And work from that Truth-

YOUR TRUTH

You Fall,
     So deeply inside yourself
Expanding from the
- - - Inside
     Out - - -
And as far as you can possibly reach!

Openly
Honestly
Powerfully-

When you Stand
Firmly-
In the Totality of

ALL

That You Are…

YOU ARE

44

☆ *Absolutely* ☆

☆ *Completely* ☆

☆ *Utterly* ☆

45

BEAUTIFUL

So,

STAND UP!

Each ONE of you

STAND UP!!

Claim Yourselves!

STAND UP!!!

AND

47

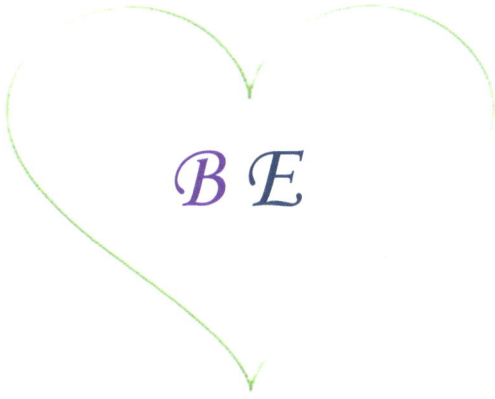

BE

BEAUTIFUL

Reviews

♥

♥Jennifer's words combined with an elegant style created an exquisite sanctuary that I just wanted to stay in forever.

-Quanah Jay Hicks, Singer/Songwriter

♥Jennifer's observation's danced down pages, the way a river winds its way across landscapes to find the ocean. Nature and spirituality are interwoven, as true beauty is conveyed with clarity of vision that reveals an understanding of the soul.

Be Beautiful invokes a simple transparency between the interconnection of the inner world and the expansive universe that nurtures it.

-Glenn Werner, Poet/Mongrel Press

♥*Be Beautiful* was an amazing inspiration to me! Jennifer reached into her heart and poured out her soul unto the pages. She brings the reader into her vision and you experience every emotion she expresses!

Be Beautiful is a page turner that you will read over and over again. It is a truly remarkable and mind-blowing book. Well Done!

-Denise Lippert, Poet

♥Jennifer read for our Rotary Club and it was met with a surprisingly touching and emotional effect for our members.

Be Beautiful is a reflection on our universal experiences of sensuality within our individual worlds as well as our reach for spiritual connection in truth, as we know and experience it.

-Dan Olson, Rotary Club

∞

Author Bio

♥

♥Jennifer is a truth seeker and artistic expressionist! She is a poet at heart and author of life. She is the published author of two other books with a fourth one in development entitled, "Poems from Passion." Jennifer has a degree in psychology and by day, serves the community as an emotional wellness coach. Jennifer is also a yoga instructor and energy therapist, offering innovative workshops in meditation, self-exploration, and healing for couples and individuals to support the greater development of their intimate, soulful selves. Currently, Jennifer is the creator and facilitator of, The Healing Project which is a community based support and learning initiative that focuses of two key aspects: Self-Discovery and Healing.

♥Along with "Be Beautiful," Ms. Circosta is a published author of her children's book, "The Many Tails of Luck-shmee" *(2011), Tate Publishing Enterprises* and her psychological thriller short story, "1713 Maplewood Drive" *(2015), Panther Productions.* Her poems have been published in seven different Anthologies and showcased in Belief Persists *(2011)* as well as Stars in Our Hearts, *(2011).* Jennifer has been chosen as a semi-finalist in the World Poetry Movement's International Competition and won the Editor's Choice Award from the International Library of Poetry for her poem, "The Maiden."

♥Jennifer has read and performed her written works throughout NYC and the Hudson Valley for nearly 20 years and is available for school events. She was the main guest speaker at Mount Saint Mary College sharing a variety of her work for the author event, "The Beauty of Words- A Writer's Journey" *(September, 2011)* and will return to the Mount, *(Novemeber, 2015*)

♥Look for Jennifer's poem, "Call Me" *(2006), Royal Fireworks* her spiritual articles, "Divine Grace" *(2008), Royal Fireworks* and "In the Presence of the Holy Spirit"*(2009), Royal Fireworks* in the spiritually driven publication, *Miracles Magazine.*

♥Jennifer strongly believes, "You are a Powerful Experience."

52

∞
53

www.ingramcontent.com/pod-product-compliance
Lightning Source LLC
LaVergne TN
LVHW010028070426
835513LV00001B/11